ICELANDIC WILDERNESS

A Photographic Journey

ICELANDIC WILDERNESS

A Photographic Journey

Daníel Bergmann

Icelandic Wilderness - A Photographic Journey
Copyright © 2003 Daníel Bergmann
www.danielbergmann.com
Translation: Martin Regal
Design: Daníel Bergmann

Printed by: Oddi hf.
Printed in Iceland

JPV Publishers, Reykjavík, 2003
www.jpv.is

ISBN 9979-775-45-9

Captions in Introduction
Page 10 An Arctic Fox in summer plumage at Hornstrandir
Page 12 Látrabjarg, the most westerly point in Europe
Page 14 An immature White-tailed Eagle
Page 15 An Icterine Warbler in 2002, the third record for Iceland
Page 16 A Long-eared Owl in Ölfus, in the fall of 2002
Page 18 An Arctic Fox of the blue variety at Hornstrandir

Acknowledgments

The photographs in this book reflect my journeys around Iceland over the past four years. They do not necessarily give an accurate view of what another traveller might see to begin with. There are no roads, no man-made constructions and no people. Just nature in its purest form.

I have consciously tried to eliminate any traces of anything that reminds one of a human presence. I visited the crater at Askja during the autumn, after the tourist season was over. That way, I had the place to myself and could direct my camera lens at whatever I pleased. I photographed the waterfall Goðafoss in a downpour and had some difficulty keeping the raindrops off the lens. No travellers have any interest in a waterfall in that kind of weather. By choosing my own locations in my own time I managed to have an innumerable number of places just to myself. Even at the famous landmark, Gullfoss waterfall, there were no people around despite it being high summer. But perhaps that is because it was four o'clock in the morning.

There are no people in these photographs but many have helped me in one way or another with compiling this book. I have travelled all over the country with Jóhann Óli Hilmarsson. He advised me on image selection and read over the text. Einar Þorleifsson, too, has been a good travel companion and is a mine of information concerning the Icelandic landscape and its fauna and flora. I want to thank both of them especially for all their assistance.

Jóhann Ísberg has been a source of invaluable advice concerning the development of the photographs, Gunnar Leifur Jónasson forwarded technical help with the processing and Björgvin Sigurðsson helped me with the layout. They, too, have my sincerest thanks.

I would like to thank Skarphéðinn Þórisson, Björn Arnarson and Árni Einarsson for providing me with accommodation on these journeys. Ornithologists, Ólafur K. Nielsen and Kristinn H. Skarphéðinsson assisted me with information concerning nest sites and the Ministry of the Environment gave its permission for me to photograph the nests of protected species.

I extend my gratitude to Ásmundur Gunnlaugsson and Lísa B. Hjaltested for their friendship over the years, and I owe a debt of gratitude to Daníel D. Bergmann and Kristbjörg Þ. Bergmann that cannot be paid. Without their support, this book would never have seen the light of day. Finally, I would like to thank Sigríður Rúna Sigurðardóttir for her unending support from the beginning to the end of this project.

Daníel Bergmann

The Puffins at Látrabjarg

Only seventy-five species of birds breed in Iceland, but the relative lack of diversity is more than compensated by the total population, which is very large indeed. It mainly comprises sea birds, ducks and waders. The sea birds are by far the most numerous, feeding on the plentiful resources of the ocean that surrounds the country. Some of them, such as auks and Fulmars and petrels come ashore in the spring to lay their eggs but spend the rest of the year out on the open sea. They nest in large and small colonies, often very densely packed together. The cliffs are literally teeming with bird-life, some of them home to millions.

One of the three largest bird-cliffs in the country is Látrabjarg, the most westerly point in Europe. It is a long, high cliff and the breeding site of possibly the most confiding Puffins in the world. The reason for this is simple: quite unlike most other areas in Iceland in which Puffins congregate, they are not hunted at Látrabjarg. They are also quite used to the visitors who come here and are little affected by their presence. The Puffin has short wings and has to flap them at great speed in order to fly, and when it lands it often looks like it is not quite going to make it. It sometimes tries to land in heavily populated areas, usually knocking a few of its companions off their feet at the same time. The Puffin is a particularly social bird and in the evenings, many of them collect together on the cliff ledges to watch the sun set and to discuss puffin-life and what they have been fishing that day. At least, that is what their behaviour suggests they are doing.

The Puffin's unusual antics make it one of the most loved birds in Iceland and many people come to Látrabjarg for the express purpose of observing it. Foreign visitors who become familiar with the Puffin find it difficult to understand how Icelanders can hunt and eat this friendly-looking creature. Personally speaking, I would not rue the disappearance of this custom. After all, modern society has enough food without having to add Puffin to the menu. Indeed, I have never actually been able to eat either Puffin or any other kind of sea bird. Some of my friends, who see this as an age-old Icelandic tradition, call me squeamish, suggesting that I am simply not nationalistic enough. I would prefer to call it respect for wildlife; but each to his own.

There are other birds beside the clever Puffin at Látrabjarg. It also holds the largest colony of Razorbills in the world, just below the steep cliff face known as Stórurð. One can also find the Common Guillemot and Brünnich's Guillemot there, sitting on the narrow ledges, huddled together in perfect harmony. There are also Fulmars and Kittiwakes to be found among them. Unlike the peaceful Guillemots, the Kittiwakes shriek and complain constantly as if they did not like each other's company. They are highly territorial and none of them alights on a strange ledge without protest from the birds settled there. The Fulmars are less aggressive but store a kind of liver-oil in their stomachs that they can spray over any intruder who comes too close to their nests.

Although the birds at Látrabjarg are in no danger from man, there are other threats. The Arctic Fox prowls around the cliff and I have seen it on bright summer nights or at the break of dawn. One time, a fox came up from the cliff with a Puffin in its jaws and when it saw me, it scurried away like a flash of lightning. On another

occasion, I was some distance from the cliff and walked past a vixen that lay in the shadows behind a rock. Just like the first fox, it did not like my presence and dashed off. I ran after it to see where it would go. It was probably one of the most stupid things I have done since there was no way I could outpace it. I once heard of a man from the east of Iceland who claimed to have been able to run up a hill faster than a fox and from that time on he was known as the "fox-beater". But after my experience on flat ground at Látrabjarg I knew that the tale had to be a tall one. Out of breath and disappointed, I watched as it paused in the distance and looked back at me. And I swear it shook its head over my stupidity before it finally ran off and disappeared from sight.

The King of Birds

When I started to take photographs of Icelandic birds in the summer of 2000, I was particularly excited about capturing some birds of prey on film. Two of them, the White-tailed Eagle and the Gyr Falcon, have a special place in the national consciousness. The White-tailed Eagle is the largest bird of prey to be found in Iceland and has been considered such a menace by many, especially Eider farmers, that it was almost made extinct. It was officially protected by a law passed in 1913 but unfortunately that did not put an end to its being shot. Yet, even more devastating was the strychnine-poisoned meat that farmers placed around their land in an effort to kill off foxes. The eagle will eat carrion on occasion and many of them were wiped out as a result. Indeed, the Icelandic Society for the Protection of Birds was founded in 1963 specifically to save the White-tailed Eagle, and with great effort finally managed to have a ban imposed on the use of poisoned carrion. Since that time the eagle population has gradually increased again.

The Gyr Falcon has always enjoyed greater respect than the White-tailed Eagle. It does not prey on Eider and will never attack lambs, as the White-tailed Eagle has certainly done on occasion. Even so, the eagle has often been wrongly accused of killing sheep, probably because it was sometimes seen eating sheep that died from some other cause.

The Gyr Falcon is a majestic bird. It is the largest falcon in the world and was in past times thought of exclusively for kings. In the eighteenth century, three hundred Gyr Falcons were taken to Denmark and the Danish crown had a monopoly over its exportation. Now, it is mainly Arab princes and oil barons who wish to acquire one. Like the White-tailed Eagle, the Gyr Falcon enjoys special protection, and anyone who wishes to approach and photograph the birds while nesting is required to apply for permission from the Ministry of the Environment. I obtained such permission first in June 2000 on condition that I selected nests in consultation with two ornithologists, Kristinn Haukur Skarphéðinsson, Iceland's leading expert on the White-tailed Eagle, and Ólafur Karl Nielsen, an expert on Gyr Falcons. Both work at the Icelandic Institute of Natural History, but I knew neither of them before I obtained permission. Kristinn Haukur told me about possible nest locations during one of our telephone conversations. He suggested one place that he thought would be best for taking photographs, and although he could not tell me the exact location he gave me a good indication of the area around it. I was not overly concerned about having precise details and set off into the unknown certain that it would be an easy enough task to find an eagle's eyrie. After all, I thought, it is a large bird.

When I arrived in the general area that Kristinn had described to me, things looked a little more complex. The rough, moss-grown lava was difficult to negotiate. I walked up and down lava covered valleys for several hours but saw no sign of any eagles. The hike across the loose ground was difficult and I took pause to lie down on the soft moss for a while. Tiny droplets of rain brushed my face and I relaxed and instantly fell asleep. When I awoke a while later I felt as rested as after a whole night's sleep. There is little as satisfying as lying in a mossy hollow under the bare sky.

As soon as I stood up, I had a strong impression about which direction I should take. I headed where my thoughts led me and reached a long, deep hollow in the lava. I stood up on a ledge there and looked out. Then, an eagle flew low along the hollow towards me. Its wingspan was greater than I had seen on any bird and my heart started to beat faster with the thrill of the sight. It settled on a small piece of lava and I walked towards it. As I approached, the eagle took to the air again and flew a little farther. I followed and it took off again. There seemed to be something strange about this behaviour. There was supposed to be a nest nearby, yet the eagle seemed totally relaxed. I decided to change my tactics and walk in the opposite direction. Then the eagle suddenly changed its tactics too. It began to squawk, flew over my head and circled above me. Finally, I spotted the nest. In it was a large fledgling eaglet. I climbed up to the cup of the nest and took a look at the eaglet. It was not afraid of me. On the contrary, it raised itself up, extended its wings and hissed at me. We looked one another in the eye.

I have, since that time, found many an eagle's nest during the summer months and sat for days on end in hides during the wintertime waiting to catch a glimpse. But the eagle has not been an easy subject. It is a nervous creature and extremely cautious. It often perches beside its nest, remaining absolutely still for hours on end. A bird of this size needs a great deal of energy to fly, as one can easily see from its laboured take off. That is why it uses thermals to glide on its broad wings and in between flights spends long periods of time as still as a statue.

Photographing the White-tailed Eagle is a test of patience. It is sensitive during the egg-laying period and one has to conceal one's presence so as to disturb the bird as little as possible. But sitting quietly in small hides for a long time can be very tedious indeed. Usually, there is little going on but one still has to keep awake in the eventuality that something might happen. Reading is out of the question and the slightest movement might alarm the subject. The summers can be extremely warm and the winters unbearably cold. I particularly remember sitting in a small wooden hide beside an eagle's winter feeding site. There was just about enough room in the cabin for me to sit but not much more. A strong wind was blowing, at least twenty metres per second, and the opening for the lens stood directly against it. It was eighteen degrees below zero, and with the combined wind-chill factor it was much colder than that. I was inside a thick sleeping bag and dressed to the hilt to keep warm. After having sat there for about five hours, having seen nothing but a group of Ravens, I gave up. I was so cold I could hardly feel any sensation in my fingers and toes anymore and I had started to shake. As I scrambled out of the hut, an eagle took flight about fifty metres away. It probably knew I was there the whole time but I was not aware of its presence until that moment. It had been perching nearby, out of my line of sight where I sat in the hut. Kristinn Haukur told me once "You have to make an effort for the eagle." Clearly, I had not done quite enough on that occasion.

I have had much better luck with the Gyr Falcon. I first met ornithologist Ólafur Karl Nielsen at Lake Mývatn in the summer of 2000. I asked him where I would find Gyr Falcon eyries. He was rather reluctant to supply me with any information to begin with and politely tried to get me to abandon my efforts. But I was determined, and in the end he told me the whereabouts of one Gyr Falcon nest. Patient as ever, Ólafur had tried to dissuade me from approaching a nest. He had learned from bitter experience of photographers and film-makers who had carelessly caused so much disturbance around Gyr Falcon nests that the parent birds stayed away for too long and their fledglings had subsequently died from exposure.

The nest that Ólafur pointed out to me proved to be one of the most amazing I have seen. Usually, the Gyr Falcon lays its eggs high up on a cliff face or in another inaccessible rocky place, but this nest was situated on a ledge on a low cliff face close to the ground. Luckily enough, the young falcons were almost large enough to fend for themselves. They had left the nest and sat on a ledge just above it. There was a grassy slope that lay below that upper ledge, where I managed to set up a portable hide. As I got myself settled there, the female Gyr Falcon flew straight at me and shrieked to show how little she cared for my presence. But once I was in my camouflaged tent, everything became quiet and still. There were four young Gyr Falcons of varying size. The largest was quite big and bold, while the smallest still had patches of down on its body. I sat there for two days and managed, among other things, to see the female bring food to its young. The male bird never brings food directly to the young. Instead, it bears it first to the female and she then takes it to them. That is how I knew it was the female feeding them. They were so large that she did not need to do much more than place the food beside them and leave. When the weather got worse with wind and rain I slowly packed up my gear and left. But I was so impressed by this family of Gyr Falcons that I came back again one week later. By then, three of the fledglings could fly. The smallest, which was not yet ready for flight, stayed close to the nest. I sat there for a while and watched it. As I was about to leave, the female arrived, circled above me a few times and then settled on a nearby rock. It was truly wonderful to see that majestic bird at such close range. I said my goodbyes, took my leave, and have not visited the place since. But the memory of the experience is still a part of me.

Face to Face with an Owl

Despite the fact that there are only seventy-five species of birds that regularly breed in Iceland, more than three hundred and fifty different species have been seen here. Some of them migrate through Iceland on the way to and from more northerly breeding grounds. Others just spend the winter here, such as the rather inappropriately named Iceland Gull. However, the great majority of species that have been seen in Iceland are vagrants, birds that are carried out of their migratory flight paths by strong winds, sometimes during the spring though more often in autumn.

Originally, my interest was only in Icelandic birds. I quickly learned to recognise most resident and migratory species, and every once in a while I spotted a bird that I could not identify at all. But over the years I have come to know more about these temporary guests and can now justifiably call

myself a birder. Even so, I do not hurry off to try to see as many different kinds as possible. If I find a stray bird, I will often spend a good deal of time observing it. Sometimes, too, I get news of a particular species and that can inspire me to go to the other side of the country to see it. For example, that is what I did when I heard there was a Great White Egret at a pond in Austur-Skaftafellssýsla, a large and pure white bird found in south-east Europe and Africa. It was only the second time this species had been seen in Iceland. I sped off in my car immediately and drove five hundred kilometres to the east of the country. When I reached the area, I slept in the car and then went off the following morning in search of the egret. I found it in a marshland near Hraunkot in Lón, where it had first been seen. I spent some considerable time making my approach and watched it as it caught a trout for breakfast. Then it flew about and I took pictures of it against snow-covered mountains—a background against which it is unfamiliar in its native range.

But the quest for vagrants is not always so exciting. Often, one finds oneself looking for small species that are barely distinguishable from one another, usually during autumn. For example, European warblers and finches that inhabit forested areas. They are mainly driven to the south coast where there are large distances between the forested areas that attract these species like a magnet. Most of these birds are naturally agile, shy and nervous, and identifying them accurately can be quite a task, let alone catching them on film.

Birding is an incurable obsession, and I had soon begun to compile a list of birds that I had seen and another of birds that I wanted to photograph. High up on this second list was the Short-eared Owl, the only owl to breed in Iceland on a regular basis. In the summer of 2002 I was determined to add the Short-eared Owl to my collection. But although I saw seven individuals in various parts of the country and knew of two nests, I did not manage to take any photographs.

In July of that year, I went with a group of people from the Institute of Natural History and a friend and fellow photographer, Jóhann Óli, on a birding expedition to Ódáðahraun, Iceland's most extensive lava field. Snowy Owls had nested there right up to 1956, although its more common habitat was and is Greenland and various other places within the Arctic Circle. Some people believe that the Snowy Owl still nests in many places in the Icelandic highlands. Individuals have been seen here every year and often in the same areas. In

1998, a nest was discovered in the West Fjords and it is therefore clear that the Snowy Owl can still be regarded as a resident nesting species, even though that residency may be irregular.

On our way to Ódáðahraun, the party stopped at a river to find a suitable crossing place. While they were doing so, I walked up a nearby lava slope. I looked at all the ledges and rocks where an owl might perch and besides one of them I found a long white feather. Ólafur Nielsen, who was with the party, confirmed that it was a Snowy Owl feather and, what was more, freshly moulted.

When we reached our destination, we saw a huge white Snowy Owl sitting on a column of lava. There was too little daylight to take photographs, so we decided to set up camp instead. The ornithologists crawled into their sleeping bags—their main task after all being to estimate the number of birds in the area. I had come, on the other hand, in the hope of seeing the owl that was waiting for me out in the lava. I dressed myself up warmly and walked all night until I found it again. It had moved a few kilometres. I approached with my head down, as I had read somewhere that the best way to approach owls was to avoid looking them in the eye. That seemed to work well enough, for although the Snowy Owl is thought to be especially cautious, this one allowed me to approach within eighty metres of where it sat. Shortly afterwards, the sun came up and I put down my tripod and took some photographs of it.

That year I also saw a Long-eared Owl for the first time. I had gone birding in the autumn, and was wandering around in some woodlands when I spotted what I first thought was a Short-eared Owl. It sat below a grass covered knoll and I was able to watch it comfortably from where I stood. Its feathered "ears" that stood up from its head and its orange eyes told me immediately that it was not a Short-eared Owl. Indeed, the Long-eared Owl was the only species it could be. It is a relatively common vagrant during the autumn months and has been known to spend the entire winter here. That year I saw three of the four species of owl that have been found in Iceland. I was captivated by the beauty they share—large, protruding eyes, a neck that can turn full circle, thick plumage, and broad wings that beat silently.

Arctic Foxes at Hornstrandir

I do not regard Hornstrandir on the north-west coast of Iceland as being entirely part of this world. It has a sense of mystery and adventure found nowhere else that I know of. There are no roads in that area so the only way to get there is to walk or to approach by sea. That is part of its wonder and attraction.

The vegetation at Hornstrandir grows wild, free from the intrusion of ever-hungry flocks of sheep. When the last farmers deserted their farms there in the middle of the last century, they took their cattle and sheep with them. What a blessing it is to be able to say that there is at least one part of the country in which one can see how lush the vegetation grows if it is left in peace.

The Arctic Fox is a protected species at Hornstrandir nature reserve. In fact, it is the true first inhabitant of the country, the only native land mammal found here, where it has survived since the last ice age, perhaps even longer. It has therefore had sufficient time to adapt itself to the Icelandic environment. Those who wish to see the Arctic Fox in its native habitat, living free from fear of human intrusion, have to go to Hornstrandir. Which is exactly what I did.

Hornvík is a deep bay, surrounded by two large bird cliffs which, together with Látrabjarg, are the three largest in the country. They are called Hornbjarg and Hælavíkurbjarg, both of them steep and imposing. I came to Hornvík by boat and stayed there for a few weeks in a tent by the shore. Each day, I walked up to Hornbjarg to be among the foxes and birds, but it took me two whole days to find the first den. I allowed the animals time to get used to my presence and eventually chose a den where the female was more relaxed than those in surrounding ones. She took to me well from the very start, circled up close to me on the second day, lay down and took a short nap. She seemed to sense that I meant her no harm.

The following day, I met her mate and, a little later, their cubs. The male was not quite as quick to accept me and kept a close eye on all my movements. I sat close to the den and watched their daily behaviour. There were only two cubs. One did not dare to go far from home, but the other went with its mother on journeys around the neighbouring area. It was fun watching the way he followed her. He was rather clumsy and his balance was not fully developed yet, resulting in a tendency to fall over forwards, and occasionally his curiosity got him into difficulties. But the female watched over him carefully. She allowed him to jump at her and play around, then tussled with him in a friendly fashion, appearing to enjoy the game as much as him. One derives so much from watching wild animals going through their daily routine. It also gives us an insight into nature itself, of which we ourselves are an integral part.

On the shore below my tent, I often saw a Harbour Seal lying on the same piece of rock. One morning, just after I awoke, I went down to the beach to stretch my legs and it looked at me with its huge eyes and seemed to be surprised to see me. But he made good company after he became used to me and seemed to quite like this strange creature that walked and hopped about on his beach.

When the boat came to fetch me at the end of my stay, the seal lay as usual on its rock. I pointed him out to the boatman and said: "May I introduce my friend, Snorri, to you." But he replied rather gruffly: "He hasn't got much time left. I'll shoot it the next time I come here. The bloody things eat way too much of our cod." I was not happy with his response but did not reply. If only people could understand that all forms of life are connected. We did not spin life's web, we are merely strands in it. If we harm the web we do harm to ourselves. That is one of the laws of the universe.

A Sense of Purpose

I have always had a strong sense of the visual and I started to take photographs as a youngster. I had a book of images from Africa, compiled by a German couple who travelled around the continent in a minivan and recorded a great deal of information about its wild fauna. I did not understand a word of the text, but the pictures spoke to me, and I dreamed of seeing it all with my own eyes. I told no one about my dream, and over the years it all became more blurred.

As a teenager I was always searching for meaning. I felt that life lacked a deeper purpose and I was burning with questions that nobody seemed to be able to answer. I was solitary and perhaps rather eccentric, and in one moment of frustration I went to see a medium. One of the first things he asked me was: "What happened to your dream of Africa?" I tensed up. How could he have known what I thought about as a child? "We are given dreams so that we can make them come true," he answered.

I had to leave Iceland and live abroad to understand my feelings about the land in which I was raised. Now, I do not wish to be anywhere else. My roots are here and they go deep. My dreams of trips to strange lands changed and I realised that the journey that mattered most to me was a journey inwards, to the heart of things. I have experienced a great deal that confirms to me that there is a higher power at work in our daily existence, and one that has generously given me yet another opportunity to take one step further towards the mysteries of the development of the soul. With gratitude, I offer this book in its honour.

A female fox of the white variety near her den in Hornvík at Hornstrandir.
The Arctic Fox is the only mammal to have inhabited the country before the arrival of man.

A Black-tailed Godwit on its nesting grounds on the Snæfellsnes peninsula. The population of this species has increased in recent decades, and it can now be found in fertile marshlands in most parts of the country.

A Puffin comes in to land at Lundabrekka on the island of Skrúður in Fáskrúðsfjörður.
This is one of the most densely populated Puffin colonies in the world.

Barrow's Goldeneye is primarily a North American bird, and Iceland is the only country in Europe in which it breeds. Lake Mývatn and the Laxá river in Mývatnssveit county are its main breeding grounds.

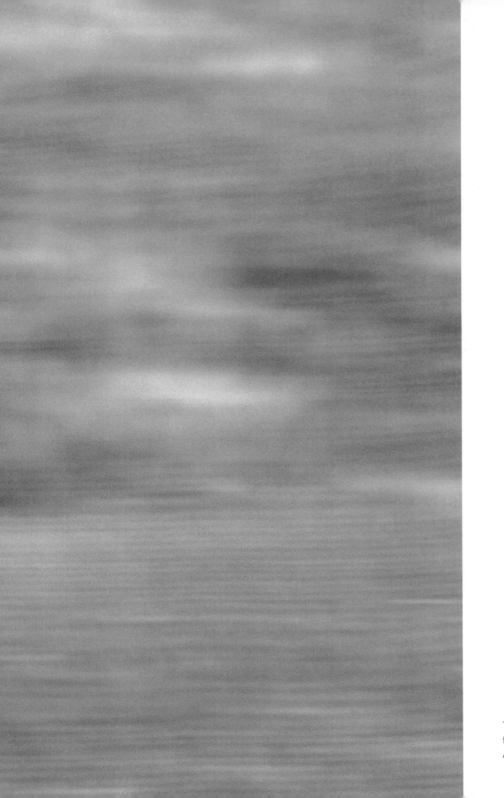

The Arctic Fox prowls its territory in search of
food and marks its perimeters to warn off rivals.
An individual of the blue variety on patrol.

The first rays of the summer sun illuminate the spray from the waterfall Gullfoss.

The morning sun picks out details on the wall of ice at the Tungnafellsjökull glacier.

Snow-covered Mt. Skjaldbreiður towers over Lake Þingvallavatn.

Great Northern Divers at Hraunlandarif on the Snæfellsnes peninsula.
Iceland is the only breeding site for this bird in the whole of Europe.

LEFT
The southern face of the Snæfellsjökull glacier is an impressive sight. The volcanic activity from within the glacier has shaped the surrounding landscape, which is now a national park.

RIGHT
The Gyr Falcon chooses a favourite spot to perch, from which it has a good view of its surroundings. A female at its nest in north-east Iceland.

The wastes of Sprengisandur. Black
sand for as far as the eye can see.

Lenticular clouds over Jarlhettur near Langjökull glacier.

An Arctic Skua takes an opportunity to cool down on a warm spring day at Lón in Austur-Skaftafellssýsla.

A stone smoothed by the surf at Festarfjall in Hraunsvík.

A herd of reindeer during the mating season in the autumn. Reindeer were imported
to Iceland in the eighteenth century. Now, they roam wild in the eastern regions.

Litla-Brandsgil at Landmannalaugar.

Hot springs at Kerlingarfjöll mountains.

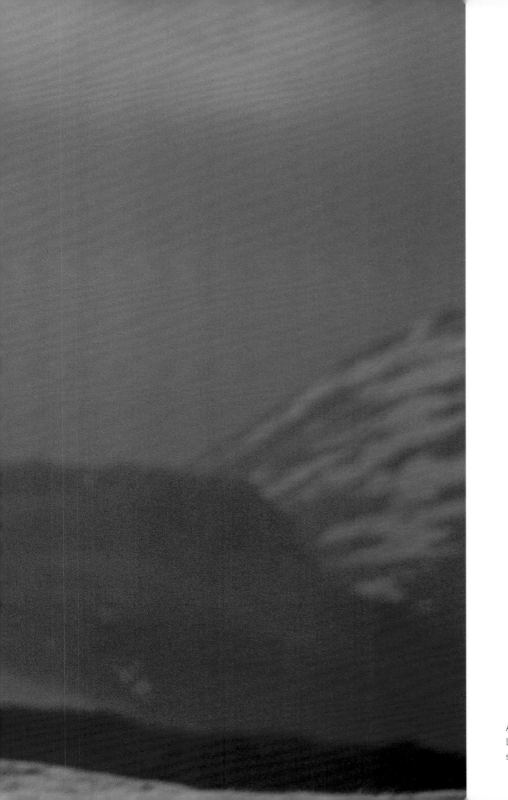

A Great White Egret in flight at Hraunkot at Lón in Austur-Skaftafellssýsla. This is only the second sighting ever in Iceland of this species.

A yawning fox at Hornbjarg at Hornstrandir.

The Iceland Gull spends the winter on the coast, but then migrates to more northern climes to breed.

A Puffin at Látrabjarg.

Harlequin Ducks in springtime on the banks of the Laxá river in Mývatnssveit.
Like the Barrow's Goldeneye and the Great Northern Diver, the main range of the
Harlequin is in North America. Iceland is the only place in Europe where it breeds.

A Horned Grebe catches some fry for its young. The Horned Grebe has declined considerably in numbers from previous times, partly because of the draining of marshlands and partly because of the arrival of the Mink.

An eruption at Mt. Hekla in February 2000.

Hornvík at Hornstrandir at sunset. The bright spots on the surface of the water are Kittiwakes fishing.

A Puffin on the edge of Látrabjarg. Nowhere else is the Puffin quite as confiding.

The Red Knot comes to Iceland in springtime and autumn on its way to and from its nesting grounds in Greenland. A flock of Red Knots at high tide at Beruvík on the Snæfellsnes peninsula.

A view down the Jökulsá river canyon. The spray comes from the Hafragilsfoss waterfall.

A high temperature thermal area in the Kerlingarfjöll mountains.

A Pink-footed Goose at its nest in Þjórsárver.

Ice floes in the glacial lagoon at Breiðamerkursandur.
The lagoon, which is about 100 metres deep, was
formed when the Breiðamerkurjökull glacier retreated.

Mt. Herðubreið, known in Iceland as the "Queen of Mountains", seen from Mt. Askja.

The Askja crater after the first autumn snow has fallen.

The waterfall Goðafoss in the Skjálfandafljót river rushes over the edge of the lava field at Bárðardalshraun.

A view from the Hofsjökull glacier over Sprengisandur.

A Red-necked Phalarope on Lake Mývatn. There are thousands of
pairs at these dense breeding grounds in Mývatnssveit county.

A flock of Sanderlings feeding in Sandgerði during the spring. A few thousand of these birds
stage at Faxaflói bay and various other areas during their spring and autumn migration.

The call of the Whimbrel is one of the characteristic sounds of an Icelandic summer.
The majority of the European Whimbrel population breeds in Iceland.

A rainbow at Ljósavatnsskarð. Birch-covered slopes in the background.

Looking northeast from Bjargtangar at Látrabjarg.
The glaciers of the ice age shaped the landscape
of the West Fjords.

Cotton grass reflected in a small pond at Hornstrandir.

The Goldcrest is one of Iceland's most recent colonists. It began breeding after an autumn influx in 1995 and has increased in numbers rapidly ever since. It can now be found in all the main woodland areas of the country. Even so, it can be difficult to spot because it is the smallest species in the whole of Europe.

The Gyr Falcon was thought to be fit only for kings in the old days. It was captured in Iceland and sent abroad to be tamed for hunting. It became totally protected in 1940.

A male Arctic Fox at Hornstrandir brings food to its den.

A female Arctic Fox playing with its cubs.

A female Gyr Falcon feeds its fledglings.

Spindly reindeer calves at Lón in Austur-Skaftafellssýsla.

Mt. Vindbelgjarfjall at Mývatn.

The northern lights over the Jökulsárlón glacial lagoon.

The glow of the midnight sun
tints the clouds and the waves.

A blue variety Arctic Fox shakes
off the water after a downpour.

A Red-throated Diver with its young in July. The Red-throated Diver is perfectly adapted for swimming and diving but not for walking. It therefore lays its eggs close to rivers, lakes and ponds, but is found most commonly close to the seashore.

A Grey Heron fishing at Heiðmörk. Several dozen Grey Herons spend the winter in Iceland and some of them can also be seen during the summer months. As far as it is known, it has never bred here.

Markarfljótsgljúfur canyon. Groundwater bursting through the walls of the canyon release small deposits of iron.

Looking southwest from Sveinstindur beside Langisjór. Substantial precipitation
in the southern highlands makes the steep slopes here fertile with vegetation.

Most Common Snipes are migratory, but the occasional individual manages to overwinter beside springs and small streams.

Like the Red-throated Diver, the Horned Grebe has difficulty walking on land because its feet are set so far back on its body, but it swims and dives all the better for that. A Horned Grebe at its nest in Mývatn.

A sea stack in Hvalvík. Mt. Snartarstaðanúpur in the background.

The Red Phalarope is a rare bird in Iceland, with fewer than a hundred pairs. It is more commonly found in the High Arctic, and Iceland is its southernmost breeding site. The Red Phalarope is one of the last migratory birds to arrive and only stays for one to two months. A male bird in a brushwood area on the south coast.

The Common Redpoll is a small member of the finch family, easily identified by the patch of red on its forehead. It is commonly found in the birch and conifer woodlands of the north and east of Iceland.

LEFT
The Svínafellsjökull glacier in Öræfasveit.

RIGHT
The waterfall Seljalandsfoss thundering
over the rock face of Eyjafjöll.

An adult Gannet on the island of Skrúður in Fáskrúðsfjörður.
The Gannet lays its eggs in dense colonies on outlying islands and rocks.

A two-year-old Gannet in flight near Skrúður island.
These birds do not attain their adult plumage until their fifth year.

An arctic riverbeauty growing on the banks on the Innri-Emstruá river. Mt. Stórkonufell in the background.

Skaftá river weaves its way through the sand flats and lava north of Lakagígar.

LEFT
The waterfall Dettifoss in the Jökulsá á Fjöllum river disappears into the shadows as twilight descends.

RIGHT
The White-tailed Eagle was hunted down in previous times and was almost at the point of extinction in the early twentieth century. It became a totally protected species in 1913 but continued to decline in numbers until poisoning sheep carcasses to kill off foxes became banned. The population has increased in size slowly since that time and there are now about fifty pairs in Iceland. The eagle is particularly sensitive during its nesting period and only about half the population manages to successfully rear its young each year.

A view of the mountains on Þríhyrningsleið track north of the Vatnajökull glacier.

Rocks and sand at Brúaröræfi.

The Eider is a sea-bird and one of the most common ducks to be found in Iceland.
Eider farmers look after their flocks, protect their nesting grounds and reap their profits from its valuable down.

Steller's Eider comes from the Arctic regions of Alaska and Siberia. It is a rare vagrant in Iceland.
Only ten individuals have been seen here. This colourful individual first joined a flock of Harlequin Ducks
at Borgarfjörður eystri in January 1998 and has been there ever since.

The Great Skua is a characteristic bird of the sands of the south coast.

Whooper Swans in flight at Þykkvabær in spring.

The Shag has a crest of feathers that it bears at the beginning of the nesting season. As the summer progresses, it loses this crest completely. Both birds were photographed at the Flateyjarklofningur in Breiðafjörður.

Hraunfossar falls on the Hvítá river at wintertime.

An immature White-tailed Eagle in its first year. A Raven flies by.

A Whooper Swan with its cygnets at the Flói nature reserve.

A fox stretches after a short nap.